Keeping Your Company Green

by Stefan Bechtel and the Editors of Rodale Press

Rodale Press, Emmaus, Pennsylvania

Printed in the United States of America on acid-free ∞, recycled paper that contains up to 10% post-consumer waste ♻

Edited by Mary V. Green

ISBN 0-87857-970-2

6 8 10 9 7   paperback

Contents

This guidebook should be considered a work-in-progress, for today's solution is far too often tomorrow's problem. Subsequent editions will be updated with new technology, new ideas and new success stories (perhaps yours?).

Prescient business leaders have named solid waste problems and environmental concerns as their most pressing business concerns of the 90s and are leading the drive for action. This is your opportunity to be proactive and take a leadership position.

If you have success stories you want to share, or are aware of products or technologies we should consider in updates of this book, please write:

Bob Teufel
President
Rodale Press
Emmaus, PA 18098

This book was inspired by the Direct Marketing Association Task Force on Environmental Issues and will be distributed at the association's Annual Conference in San Francisco's Moscone Center, the *first* Green conference held at the Moscone.

The Green Decade

- According to the marketing firm Michael Peters Group, 89 percent of U.S. consumers say they are concerned about the environmental impact of the products they buy, and 78 percent say they're willing to pay more for products that are "environmentally benign."
- "Green products will be to the 1990s what 'lite' products were to the 1980s," says Ray Goldberg, a professor of business at Harvard Business School.
- In a supplement to the 1989 annual report from Ben & Jerry's Homemade, along with all the talk of cash flow, shareholder equity and long-term debt obligations, there's a 21-point list of what's being done to cut down on "the company wastestream."
- Dozens of publicly-held corporations face a "green revolution" in the form of shareholder initiatives. Of the 300 social-issue resolutions submitted for shareholder approval at U.S. companies in 1989, 45 dealt with environmental issues.
- There are even green TV shows in the works. Ted Turner will soon unveil an animated action adventure called Captain Planet and the Planeteers, starring a sort of Indiana Jones of the environment.

Instead of Darth Vadar and his interstellar hordes, Captain Planet's new archenemies are greedy corporate polluters.

The signs are everywhere: We've entered the Green Decade. No other worry of our time seems to be as widely shared or as deeply felt, as current fears over the fate of the ailing earth. Our little planet's fragility, and its loveliness, were poignantly brought home to us in pictures beamed back from space a few decades ago. But since that time, other images have superceded that swirling, luminous portrait from space. Images of The Barge That Could Find No Home, roaming up and down the East Coast with its putrefying load of used diapers, kitchen scraps, fast-food packages, plastic toys and all the other detritus of civilization. Images of medical waste and sewage washing ashore in New Jersey. Images from newly-liberated Eastern Europe— environmental nightmares come true—of radioactive lakes, and towns so saturated with industrial soot that everything in them is absolutely black.

Although we're all to blame, corporations are often perceived to be the worst environmental offenders. With their vast resources, their access to capital and labor, businesses seem to have an almost godlike power to destroy the natural world. But they also have a godlike power to create a better world.

What will *your* company do to live more lightly on the Earth and bring about that better, greener world? How will *you* respond to consumers who express concern about the environmental impact of the products they buy, and the environmental records of the businesses they deal with? Will you stonewall, prevaricate and blame it all on tree-huggers and loonies? Will you do nothing, hoping the "green revolution" will just go the way of pet rocks and lava lamps? Or will you become a torchbearer of our passage into a new world—a world that's cleaner, safer, more productive and more sustainable?

This little book is a compendium of simple, doable steps your company can take to help keep itself— and the world—green. Most of the ideas you find here won't cost your company anything, and many will actually save you money. (Trees are green, and so are profits.) They're drawn from the experience of American businesses that are already leading the way— companies like Patagonia, Ben & Jerry's, Smith & Hawken, Seventh Generation, Rodale Press, L. L. Bean, even Procter & Gamble, Coca Cola and McDonald's.

These companies are seeking to learn a new corporate ethos. Like wilderness trekkers, they are learning to practice "low impact camping" on the planet, minimizing the waste they leave behind them. They are practicing a new vow of reciprocity, returning to the Earth at least some of what the Earth has given them. And they've learned to take a longer view of time. We've gotten where we've gotten partly due to our corporate devotion to quarterly profits—time in the short term. But in order to survive into the twenty-first century—or the twenty-fifth or the thirtieth— businesses need to take a longer, slower view of their place on the Earth. Alan Newman, the innovative direct marketer of "products for a healthy planet," named his company Seventh Generation after an old Iroquois saying: "In our every deliberation, we must consider the impact of our decisions on the next seven generations." For too long, companies have been obsessed only with their impact on the next four months. For too long, the only thing we've left for the seventh generation is our trash.

The Green Consumer

And what a mind-boggling load of trash we've left! Every year, in America, businesses and individuals throw away 160 million tons of junk—that's 3½ pounds a day for every man, woman and child. Landfill sites in the United States are filling up, and being shut down, at a rate of about one a day. On almost every environmental front, we seem to have reached the brink of crisis: solid waste, air quality, acid rain, ozone depletion, water quality, deforestation. It's hard to overestimate the gravity of our present situation. The World Wildlife Fund estimates that in 1990, species are disappearing at a rate of about one per hour. Though not all scientists agree that "global warming" is a genuine phenomenon, the fact remains that the five hottest years ever recorded occurred during the 1980s. And the tropical rain forests, those vast pharmacopoeias of medicinal plants and undiscovered animal species, are being destroyed at the rate of one square mile every 15 minutes.

Thomas Lovejoy, a biologist for the Smithsonian Institution, recently offered a frightening prediction to the American Institute of Biological Sciences: "I am utterly convinced that most of the great environmental struggles will be either won or lost in the 1990s. And that by the next century it will be too late."

Many American corporations, like the ones described in this book, have risen to the challenge of these great environmental struggles. But in many ways, it's the American consumer who's led the way. In poll after poll, they've expressed their concern about the deterioration of the environment, and their willingness to choose—and pay more for—products, packaging and services that will protect it. Consumer polls have also revealed something of vital importance to marketers: The most critical segment of consumers are the ones most likely to be concerned about the environment. Gallup polls have shown that the typical "green" consumer is likely to be a well-educated, affluent woman between the ages of 25 and 49, who is married and has children. In other words, your best customer.

But if this affluent, well-educated green consumer doesn't affect the way you do business, lawmakers soon will. There are legislative initiatives on the dockets in all 50 states, attempting to encourage the production of more "green" consumer goods. Recycling is now mandatory in 9 states, and pending in 22 others. And many other states are considering laws that regulate the use of recycled or recyclable materials in packaging.

"Environmental pressures on corporations can only get tighter in the 1990s," says Raymond J. Carlisle, a senior business consultant at SRI International. "Leading corporations are beginning to acknowledge this and realize they can control their own destinies by acting before someone forces them."

But it's not only consumers and legislators who are forcing the hand of business—so is the mess we've made. "This time the issue is not simply our consciences telling us to do the right thing for the world," says Robert Teufel, president of Rodale Press and chairman of the Direct Marketing Association's Environmental Task Force. "This time, the economic and financial issues of solid waste disposal and closing landfills are forcing awareness and change. Our environmental concerns are largely the result of being inundated by our own trash."

It's Cheaper Being Green

Sure, being green is the right thing to do. But businesses have begun to discover something else, too: It's usually cheaper. And often it's cheaper not just in the long term but *now*. Setting up an in-house recycling system cuts down your trash-hauling fees and generates cash through the sale of glass, aluminum and paper. Installing low-flow toilets or compact flourescent lights saves on water and electricity. And, of course, the best way to avoid the environmental horror and crippling expense of a toxic dump site cleanup is not to make one in the first place.

Making a genuine effort to keep your company green can have other benefits that are less tangible but equally real. "I know companies that never dreamed their button-down staffs would get excited about a recycling program—but believe me, it happens," says Alan Newman of Seventh Generation. A genuine corporate commitment to the environment engenders loyalty on the part of the staff, and helps reduce employee turnover. It also helps you recruit top people. "Your staff will see it as a fringe benefit," says Newman. "That may be hard for some people to believe, but that's the way the world is moving these days." And a happier staff, with lower turnover, saves you money.

And, of course, becoming aggressively green will not go unnoticed by your customers. They're looking to differentiate between the companies they do business with, and a company that stands out is one they're likely to patronize.

You shouldn't feel overwhelmed by the task of "greening" your company—or too terribly self-righteous if you've already started. We're all relatively new to this. Even the most innovative companies didn't institute company-wide recycling programs much more than a few years ago. Many of the bright green initiatives you'll read about here are still "pilot programs" or "under corporate review," or "soon to be implemented." We've all made dumb mistakes, and will probably make more. (One ad agency, flushed with self-righteousness, printed up stickers touting its in-house recycling program. Unfortunately, they were printed on coated paper that couldn't be recycled!)

The purpose of this little book is to help you get started somewhere. There are dozens of ideas presented here, but you don't have to try them all. Try picking just five. Start somewhere. Do something. Saving the world might be easier than you think.

The Great Wall of Paper

This is supposed to be the Electronic Age, but no business in America could operate without paper. Even fax machines, our latest technological addiction, generate a regular Niagara Falls of paper (much of it heavily treated with chemicals and difficult or impossible to recycle). In fact, it's been estimated that the average American office worker chucks a pound and a half of paper every day. As a nation, businesses and individuals throw away enough office and writing paper every year to build a 12-foot wall between Los Angeles and New York.

But in the new, greener world we're entering— more complex, more crowded, more endangered— businesses need to pay closer attention to the vast, disorderly paper trail they're leaving behind them. Paper itself—that wondrous, world-changing stuff— can no longer be taken for granted. The whiteness of the sheet you hold in your hand can no longer be taken for granted. (Was it bleached using an acid-free process, or did the whiteness come from chlorine bleaching, which produces toxic dioxins?) Was it recycled, or was it made from "virgin" fiber? If it was recycled, how much came from so-called "post-consumer" waste— stuff people actually dumped in the trash? (Very often, only 10 or 15 percent—if any at all—actually comes from bona fide post-consumer wastepaper, the discarded catalogues, old newspapers and love letters that wind up in landfills. And only by cutting down on post-consumer waste do we save forests and reduce the deluge of solid waste entering our landfills.) What was the entire "life cycle" of the paper your company is using, from the trees it took to produce the pulp, to the water and energy it took to run the mills, to the by-products produced by its manufacture, to the place it will go when you or your customers are through with it?

Sure, asking these sorts of questions is a bit of a bother at first. But that's just a sign of the times. Shortly before he left office, Ed Koch, former mayor of New York, signed a contract to replace the city's 1.4 million yellow legal pads with white ones, which are easier to recycle. He was returning to a private law practice, and he couldn't help but grumble a little. "These are *legal* pads," he groused to the *New York Times*. "Now they'll think we're doctors!"

Sorry, Ed. You'll get used to it.

What You Can Do:

Once is not enough. Make it a habit to use both sides of a piece of paper whenever you can. Get a two-sided copier machine. Or if you don't have one, make copies on the back side of paper that's already been used for something else (at least when you don't have to impress anybody with the result.) Try to use both sides of a piece of paper before tossing it into the "recycle" basket under your desk. In company publications, from direct mail packages to letters, try to print on both sides of the page whenever possible.

Don't repeat yourself too often. Try to cut down on the number of copies of things you make for inter-office distribution. Use routing slips or voice mail rather than multiple copies of things. Think: "Does he/she *really* need a copy of this?"

Don't waste it, use it. Use wastepaper for scratch paper.

Cut down on memos. You can reduce the number of company-wide memos by publishing a weekly in-house newsletter that incorporates personal news.

Recyfile. The innovative Texas ad agency, GSD&M, sent out memos to remind everyone on staff to reuse file folders, Pendaflex files, paper clips, poster and mounting board, notebooks, divider tabs and envelopes. They followed up with a weekly reminder in the in-house newsletter.

Suck a mug. You can cut down on paper use and cut costs at the same time by eliminating throwaway plates and utensils in company cafeterias. Rodale Press employees are encouraged to buy ceramic mugs with ceramic lids, instead of using paper cups for their coffee. The mugs are sold at cost, saving employees a nickel for every cup of java, saving the company the cost of disposing of the cups and saving the landfills the additional burden.

A few years ago, Patagonia, the outdoor specialty company, discovered it was spending $12,000 a year on paper cups alone. So Tim Sweeney, the company's environmental resource coordinator, stopped buying paper cups, plates and plastic utensils for company cafeterias, and now saves the corporation thousands a year. Cutting out throwaways required installing small, under-the-counter dishwashers at several of the company's smaller locations, but Patagonia still came out ahead, Sweeney says. (Not to be dissuaded from going all the way, Sweeney even found a source— a local janitorial supply place—for skinny little wooden stir sticks, to replace the non-biodegradable plastic ones they had been using.)

Seventh Generation does something else to cut down on fast-food paper and plastic waste: Twice a week, the company orders in lunch. A local company provides cheap, tasty food, which is consumed on the premises on washable plates with reusable utensils. Eating-in also conserves the gas that would have been burned by all those single-passenger cars dispersing through town—and besides, the staff enjoys sitting down together like that every once in a while. (Hey, isn't this what the whole world used to do for lunch about 50 years ago?)

Use me, abuse me, but don't throw me away! Use cloth towels instead of paper ones in the company kitchen and bathrooms.

Recycled Paper: Getting Better and Cheaper

Consider this: According to Conservatree Paper Company, a California-based wholesaler of recycled paper products, every ton of recycled paper:

● Conserves about 17 trees.

- Saves about 4,100 kilowatts of energy—enough to power the average home for six months.
- Saves 7,000 gallons of water.
- Keeps almost 60 pounds of pollution effluents out of the air.
- Eliminates about 3 cubic yards of trash, and reduces the need for more landfills.
- Turns "trash" into valuable resources.

It's not as if recycled paper were some outlandish new idea. In fact, until fairly recently, *all* paper was recycled. Modern paper was the brainchild of a second-century Chinese inventor named Ts'ai Lun, who made his first batch out of old rags, used fishing nets, hemp and China grass. Fifteen hundred years later, in 1690, when the first paper mill in America opened for business near Philadelphia, paper was still made mostly out of old cotton and linen rags. It wasn't until the late 1800s that mills figured out a way to use wood fiber to make paper, and production exploded. Today, after a binge of unprecedented proportions, we're just beginning to recover our senses. Americans now recycle about 28 percent of the paper we consume, which isn't too bad, but we could do better. In Europe, the recycling rate is around 35 percent, and in Japan and Taiwan, folks recycle over half of their wastepaper.

Things are changing fast, though. In governments and corporations, signs of change abound:

- The U.S. Government Printing Office, responding to the Resource Conservation and Recovery Act, now requires a minimum of 50 percent recycled fiber in all its printed products.

- Washington, D.C., paper-shuffling capital of the world, recently passed a city ordinance requiring offices and businesses to separate white paper from colored paper.
- In Canada, the city of Toronto has passed an ordinance making it illegal to sell a newspaper through a vending machine unless it's printed on recycled paper.
- In terms of volume if not in value, wastepaper is the port of New York and New Jersey's biggest export. In 1988, 938,269 tons were shipped overseas, the *New York Times* reports.
- Red Cavaney, president of the American Paper Institute, says the paper industry will have the capacity to process all kinds of paper recycled in America by 1995. The industry's goal: To recycle 40 percent of all paper consumed in the United States by 1995, or 40 million tons. Forty million tons: In bales 5 feet long, 4 feet high and 3 feet wide, that would wrap 1½ times around the Earth at the equator—a sort of globe-girdling chastity belt for a civilization just learning to control its appetites.

Many companies are looking into the feasibility of using recycled papers wherever possible, or are already doing so. Direct marketers and organizations like The Body Shop, World Watch Institute and Greenpeace already print their direct mail materials on recycled paper. Of the 2.6 million books Rodale Press published during the last half of 1989, half were printed on recycled paper. The company also now uses recycled paper for its phone message pads, envelopes, and stationery. Even the *Encyclopaedia Britannica* and the best-seller *Iaccocca* are printed on recycled paper.

But Rodale Press and many other well-intentioned marketers are now facing a vexing dilemma: The technology has not quite caught up with everyone's good intentions. While lower grades of recycled paper, like newsprint, memo pads or copy paper, may actually be cheaper than paper made of virgin fiber, higher grades—especially glossy, clay-coated magazine stock—are still considerably more expensive. It's easy to talk about keeping your company green, but this is where the rubber really meets the road.

"If we told people that we were going to charge an extra 25 percent to save trees and protect the environment, they'd say they were going to another printer," says one production manager of a small printing company.

One other big problem: Recycled glossy paper still cannot quite match the quality of glossy paper made from virgin fiber. Because recycled paper tends to be fairly rough and porous, applied ink tends to spread, so color photographs don't reproduce as crisply. It also tends to lack the tensile strength of old-fashioned paper, so it sometimes comes apart during the printing process, gumming up the presses.

The Sierra Club has taken considerable heat from its members because, while the Club's nonpictorial books, notecards and greeting cards are printed on recycled paper, its crisp, lustrous nature calendars are not. In a recent note to readers in *Sierra* magazine, Club executive Douglas Scott expressed the Club's commitment to the goal of printing the 1992 calendars on recycled stock—once high-quality, glossy paper made of substantially recycled fiber becomes available.

The technology is changing, and changing fast. Why? Because governments and businesses have led the way, creating a demand that mills are hastening to fill. It's plain old capitalist economics, as American as apple pie and Adam Smith: When the demand is there, new suppliers, and new technologies, will emerge.

"We're selling all we can make at this point," a senior sales rep for Simpson Paper said recently. "Almost daily, mills are introducing different recycled grades. Everyone is jumping on the bandwagon." Adds a rep from Georgia-Pacific: "I used to get one or two phone calls a week about recycled paper. Now, I get ten a day. The primary interest in the past year was initially from government printers and people who were forced to work within government requirements. Now, we're seeing private sector usage growing, and it's growing every month with environmentally concerned Fortune 1,000 companies."

Now recycled paper manufacturers are poised to leap the final hurdle: producing high-quality, competitively-priced glossy paper for magazine publishing. In September 1989, a small conservation magazine in Iowa became perhaps the first magazine in America to be printed on glossy, recycled paper. *Iowa Conservationist* reported that the paper in its September issue was made of 40 percent recycled paper waste, including 10 percent "post-consumer" wastepaper— the real dreck, the discarded envelopes, office paper and packaging that make up about half of all the garbage in landfills. Reusing post-consumer waste is the only thing that really saves forests and cuts down on solid waste in landfills. (Most recycled papers have very little post-consumer waste in them, if any. Ask your supplier about the pre- and post-consumer fiber content of the paper you're buying.) Their supplier: Future Fibers, of San Raphael, California, who've developed a recycled stock that the company claims prints as well as any of the non-recycled papers. When fed through the printer's sophisticated web press, it ran perfectly with no adjustments, the publisher reported. It was still considerably more expensive, however: Using recycled paper raised the magazine's printing costs by more than 13 percent.

Other publishers and marketers have also taken the plunge. *Greenpeace* magazine, *Garbage* magazine, and color catalogues from Seventh Generation, The Body Shop, Esprit de Corps, Smith & Hawken and Patagonia are all printed on recycled paper. Patagonia, whose oversized, gloriously photographed catalogue is one of the most beautiful in the business, estimates that by using recycled paper, the company saved 14,500 trees, 6 million gallons of water, 3.5 million kilowatt hours of energy, and kept 1,560 cubic yards of solid waste out of the landfills. And Smith & Hawken's Ted Tuescher figured out that the number of kilowatt hours of energy the company will save by using recycled paper in 1991 could provide enough power to send the company's electric car around the Earth at the equator 671 times.

What You Can Do:

Start from the bottom. To start your company's switch to recycled papers, it's probably easiest to begin with fairly rough-grade, uncoated papers like toilet tissue, paper towels, and copy paper. Rodale Press started out by buying all recycled interoffice memo pads. You can also use recycled paper for computer reports, company stationery and letterhead, phone pads and plain-paper fax machines—which are sometimes cheaper than other brands made from virgin fiber. Rodale discovered it could get recycled toilet tissue 28 percent cheaper than the old "virgin" stuff they were using. (Source: James River Paper in Richmond, Virginia.) Lower-grade papers also tend to use more post-consumer wastepaper. For instance, Fort Howard Paper Company's "Envision" line of recycled papers includes toilet tissue made from 100 percent post-consumer waste. Can't do much better than that. It's a little gray, and a little rough, but who cares? In the 1990s, gray toilet paper means you're green.

(The ultimate minimum-impact paper is paper that's 100 percent recycled post-consumer waste that has not been de-inked or bleached, meaning that less water and fewer chemicals are needed to make it. What do you get in the end? Gray paper.)

You've heard of green tea—try green coffee. Those dazzling-white paper filters used at the company coffee trough are probably bleached with chlorine, which produces dioxins. Why not switch to unbleached filters? Several companies are now marketing coffee filters that either eliminate chlorine from the paper-making process entirely (these tend to be brown), or use an oxygen-whitening process that cuts back on the chlorine.

Close the window. Those little plastic "window" envelopes are cute and useful, but they're also hard to recycle. Also, the manufacture of plastic produces some questionable by-products. Smith & Hawken is in the process of switching to either open windows or windows made from glassine, a cellulose-based material that's completely biodegradable.

Try to become part of the solution, not the problem. Even if your company cannot yet see its way clear to buy glossy, coated paper in recycled stock— and the truth is, very few companies have—you may be able to invest in the future anyway. At *Mother Jones* magazine, the company uses recycled paper wherever they can, but they still don't use it for the magazine itself. Still, they've struck a productive compromise: They buy paper from Conservatree Paper Company, a recycled paper wholesaler which is committed to the development of new recycled products. That way, says associate publisher David Assmann, "we get good prices and service, and they use the broker's commission they earn to develop new recycled products and promote recycling. If we can't yet use recycled glossy paper, we want our dollars to go toward developing it."

Green Marketing

"Stop Junk Mail!" shrieks an ad in an environmental magazine. "Every day Americans receive enough junk mail to heat 250,000 homes. . . .Every household in America could save 1½ trees per year by eliminating their junk mail. . ." and so on. It's a dismal litany with which many Americans have now become familiar.

On the other hand, direct marketing certainly has its place. Thousands of worthy organizations, including many environmental groups, use direct mail to rally support and raise money for their causes. Millions of people shop through catalogues, thereby saving the energy they would have wasted driving to the mall. And all other forms of marketing—billboards, radio and TV advertising, extravagant promotions—consume resources and produce a certain amount of waste.

If your company does use direct marketing, you have a real obligation to do everything possible to minimize paper waste, target mailings carefully, reduce the number of packages sent to undeliverable addresses, and so on. If your catalogue winds up in the trash, it really is "junk mail." But if it winds up in the hands of someone who wants it and uses it, it's a job well done.

What You Can Do:

Use the DMA "Nixie" and "Pander" files in your merge/purge. If you're in direct marketing, you probably already know what that means, and you probably already do it. But the point is that direct marketers need to *do better* in reducing the amount of unwanted or undeliverable mail they send out. These so-called "suppression" files, when they're run against the lists you buy for your mailings, will eliminate bad, undeliverable addresses (the "nixie" file) and people who are likely to leave their bills unpaid (the "pander" file). Also, of course, direct marketers need to eliminate the names of people who have contacted the Direct Marketing Association's Mail Preference Service, indicating that they want to be taken off your list. By being prompt and conscientious in these areas, marketers can reduce their paper waste, save trees, and respect the rights of customers.

Purge your files often. Also make regular use of NCOA—the National Change of Address data bank—to purge your house files of undeliverable addresses.

Say it better, less often. "This is heresy in the direct mail business—and we're still just testing the idea—but we've decided to ask customers how many of our catalogues they want to receive every year," says Alan Newman, president of the direct marketer Seventh Generation. Many direct marketers mail their customers a catalogue eight or ten times a year. But

Seventh Generation decided to ask if they'd prefer getting one each season (a total of four), twice a year, or none at all. The company is even testing an alternative to the catalogue: a special order form which explains why the customer is not receiving the catalogue, and how to get one quickly and easily if they want it.

Can you make the content and targeting of your direct mail package so much more effective that you don't have to drop as large a mailing? Is there any way you can reduce the amount of paper you mail by cutting down on your renewal or billing series?

Use the phone. Can you make better use of the telephone? "Telemarketing plays a big role in our Christmas promotions, and it bypasses the whole paper and postage issue," says Rodale Press Corporate Subscriptions Director Ed Fones.

Shrink it. Is it possible to reduce your paper use by reducing the trim size of your catalogue or direct mail package? The U.S. Postal Service may soon *force* you to get small anyway. Beginning next year, the USPS will start adding a surcharge for handling oversized mail. Rodale Press is already testing downsized direct mail packages, says Fones. Rodale has also made an effort to cut down on the number of pages in the premium booklets sent out with new subscriptions.

Detox your mail

According to Allen Herskowitz of the Natural Resources Defense Council, a leading authority on the effect of environmentalism on business, virtually all direct marketers could "detoxify the mail" without suffering any serious financial consequences. Herskowitz suggests that companies:

- Eliminate chlorine-bleached paper from promotional pieces. (Chlorine produces dioxins.)
- Eliminate the use of plastic "polywrap" wherever possible.
- Reduce the use of heavy metals in inks.

Ordinary inks produce toxic byproducts when they're produced and are still toxic when they're disposed of. The worst offenders are shiny, metallic-looking golds, silvers and bronzes, and extremely bright yellows and reds, which take their brassy color from heavy metals in the pigments. A greener alternative: soy- or water-based inks, which are much less toxic (though they still use pigments made from petrochemicals to ensure consistency of color from batch to batch). Soy-based inks even have some advantages: They last longer, have better gloss, clean up more easily and produce fewer and less-toxic fumes than petrochemical-based inks. There are also limitations, of course—they work better with newspaper and sheet-fed presses, but have not yet been developed for the presses on which most catalogues and magazines are printed. Still, if marketers create the demand, the technology to solve all those problems is sure to follow.

Plastic: Here Today, Here Tomorrow

It's a little ironic that plastics, which characterize our whole disposable culture, have proven to be the hardest kind of waste to dispose of. But it's true: Many of the most environmentally concerned companies still haven't found a totally satisfying way to deal with their plastic wastes (except cutting back on their use of plastics in the first place.)

Using "recyclable" plastics is—at least for now—only a partially-satisfying solution, because the term is meaningless unless there's a recycler in your town who will take the stuff. In most municipalities, there isn't (at least not yet). The result is that less than 2 percent of all plastic is recycled. The introduction of "degradable" plastics offered a glimmer of hope a few years back, but recently these products, which use cornstarch-based additives to hasten their breakdown by sunlight or bacteria, have come under withering fire from environmentalists. In the anaerobic tomb of a landfill, where most of these products actually wind up, they just don't degrade as readily as their manufacturers originally claimed. Now even the manufacturers themselves admit that degradable plastics don't offer any real solution to the solid waste crisis.

Yet plastics continue to pose a serious hazard to the environment, partly because they're so good at their job: being cheap, durable, and multi-talented. The problems begin during manufacturing. Of the six chemicals whose production creates the most toxic waste, five are heavily used in the manufacture of plastics, the EPA has reported. Another problem: There are so many different kinds of plastics—46 different resins in a staggering variety of chemical formulations—that recycling them is extremely difficult. Because they're made from extremely long-chain polymers too large to be munched by microorganisms, they're practically indestructible. And, because they're so widely used, they make up an enormous amount of the wastestream. Although estimates vary, one industry analyst has estimated that plastics make up about 7 percent of the solid-waste stream by weight, 30 percent by volume and 40 to 50 percent of the litter.

There may be some good news in the offing, though. Fascinating research is currently underway at the University of Massachusetts on the production of truly biodegradable "natural plastics." These substances are made by a fermentation process similar to brewing beer, in which microorganisms are fed on glucose made from corn or wheat starch (no petroleum products required). The resulting plastic can be used to make bottles, bags and film using existing technology. It's stable in storage, and it doesn't break down until it comes in contact with soil or another bacteria-rich medium, in which case it disintegrates to carbon dioxide and water within a matter of days. It sounds too good to be true, and it is: At the moment, these experimental plastics cost 30 times as much as existing varieties. But with commercial demand, all that may change.

At the same time, the recycled plastics business is booming. In fact, industry experts have predicted that by 1995, more than 50 percent of plastic soft-drink bottles and 25 percent of food packaging will be recycled. Robert Bennett, associate dean of engineering at the University of Toledo, estimates that the roughly $50 million plastics-recycling market could be worth $340 million by 1994. Says *U.S. News & World Report*: "If the movie *The Graduate* were made today, the suburban sage would have two words to say to Dustin Hoffman: "Recycled plastics."

Let's hope so.

What You Can Do:

Should you bag the bag? For now, though, there are still some vexing problems with plastic. Typical of the environmental concerns facing marketers is the ongoing debate over the use of "biodegradable" plastic polywrap for magazines or catalogues sent through the mail. The practical advantages are many: Polywrap helps ensure that the publication will arrive in better condition, and allows marketers to mail other things (like renewal notices and promotions) without paying additional postage.

But is biodegradable polywrap really any better for the Earth than the old kind? Several years ago, convinced that it was, Rodale Press decided to switch to biodegradable polywrap for all its magazines—despite a 16 percent increase in price. The company needed to "put our money where our mouth is," said one top manager.

But since that time, a whole new wave of doubts and questions about degradable plastics has emerged, making what once seemed like a principled decision seem ever more questionable. In December of 1989, for instance, six environmental groups issued a controversial report on degradable plastics, claiming that they were "one of the biggest consumer hoaxes to come along." Said Dr. Richard Dennison, a coauthor of the Degradable Plastics Report: "The concern is that if people think you can toss plastic away and it magically disappears, they will just toss it away."

Degradable plastics just don't break down in landfills very rapidly, the report maintains. And, when they do, there are still questions about the intermediate breakdown products which are produced as the long-chain polymers degrade. (Many of the more basic components of plastic, called monomers, are known to be toxic.) Degradable plastics could cause trouble for the infant plastic recycling business, because products made from degradable plastics (like lumber and shipping pallets) are weaker and perform less well than products made from virgin resins. And there's another problem, too: Says Dr. Daryl Ditz, a researcher at the Cornell Waste Management Institute, "Degradability could put a silver bullet in the heart of recycling." Who's going to bother to recycle plastic bleach bottles, if they think they'll just vanish in a landfill?

Still, many marketers have chosen to continue using biodegradable polywrap for the time being, considering it a better alternative than nondegradable plastic wrap or no wrap at all. Other publications, including

Harrowsmith, The New Yorker and *Mother Jones*, have chosen to bag the bag.

Try paper. Is it possible you could wrap your magazine or catalogue in ordinary brown paper instead of polywrap? Rodale Press is now testing brown kraft paper "belly bands," with notices and promotions attached, instead of polywrap. *Vermont Magazine* and others have already switched to paper.

Can you "close the loop"? At Patagonia, the direct marketer of outdoor clothing and equipment, the problem is not polybagged magazines but plastic-bagged clothing. So far the company has found no satisfactory substitute for the plastic bags, which protect clothing from dampness and stains. Instead, they're trying to hammer out an ingenious "closed loop" solution. The bags are manufactured by Tacoma, Washington—based Poly Bag, which ships them to Patagonia. Patagonia in turn uses them to wrap clothing, then ships them out to 650 retail dealers. The company is now trying to set up a nationwide reclamation program, in which the dealers would then ship the used bags back to the manufacturer, who would melt them down and make more bags . . . which would then be shipped to Patagonia. "We'd basically be buying the same materials over and over," says Patagonia environmental resources director Tim Sweeney. "It's still just a pilot program, but the dealers seem enthusiastic, and we're really hoping it's going to work."

Learn to love a pet. Not all plastics are equal; some are more recyclable than others. At the moment, two of the most recyclable kinds of plastic products are those made from PET (polyethylene terephthalate) or HDPE (high-density polyethylene) resins. (How can you tell? Many plastic containers are now marked on the underside with a recycling logo and letters indicating what they're made of. If it's made of HDPE, it will say HDPE.) According to Gretchen Brewer of Earth Circle, a Massachusetts-based plastics recycling consulting firm, PET is the most recyclable resin right now—about 20 percent of PET containers are recycled, compared with less than 2 percent of other plastics. The reason: There's a strong secondary market for these resins, because plants have been designed to reuse them. A company in Michigan, for instance, is now working with Procter & Gamble to recycle PET containers for new containers of Downy, Tide and Cheer.

Maybe your recycler won't take all kinds of plastic. But what about PET and HDPE?

Take it back. Any way you could set up a system to take back the plastic packaging your product went out in? Mobil Chemical, one of the largest producers of plastic bags, will soon launch a program to recycle plastic grocery bags. It plans to work with supermarkets, beginning with 244 Safeway stores, to set up recycling programs for the collection of sacks brought back by customers. Similar programs are being set up in many other grocery store chains.

Be clever. Ben & Jerry's had a real problem figuring out a way to dispose of the 100,000 5-gallon plastic buckets in which ice cream ingredients were delivered to them. But the company's environmental director, Gail Mayville, finally came up with a solution. The buckets are now sent to Vermont Republic

Industries, a nonprofit outfit which employs the disabled. VRI cleans and shreds the buckets, then sends the result off to be remade into wastebaskets, reusable shopping containers, loose-leaf binders and key rings—some of which are sold in Ben & Jerry's gift shop.

Be honest. The degradable plastic question is just one area where there's simply no totally comforting solution available yet. So the best approach is to stay on top of emerging technologies, and keep your customers informed about your efforts. In the meantime, be honest. Do the best you can, but don't lie. Nothing is worse than fake greenery. REI, the giant consumer cooperative of sports and outdoor equipment, found a nice way to deal with the dilemma. Recently the company started sending out its catalogues in a degradable plastic bag, with the following plainspoken little note attached:

"This bag is made of a biodegradable material. REI does not bag catalogues to protect them. Bagging multiple catalogues saves paper, reduces postage costs, and makes more efficient use of the USPS transportation system. REI feels that biodegradable plastic is neither a perfect nor a final solution. It is one option among the many difficult choices an environmentally aware company has to make. Recycling is another option."

Who could argue with that?

Packaging: Reduce It, Recycle It, Refill It, Reuse It

A well-known food company recently marketed one of its famous breakfast cereals in a 15 percent larger box, with the words "New, Larger Size!" emblazoned across the side. There was just one problem: The amount of cereal in the box had increased by less than 2 percent. The "new, larger size" contained mostly high-priced air.

Not so long ago, this cardboard embodiment of smoke and mirrors was standard practice among marketers. But those days may be numbered. For one thing, as a society we can no longer afford it. A third of the junk that winds up in landfills (not to mention junk along the highways) is packaging. For another, consumers are becoming increasingly concerned about the foolishness and waste of goods packaged in oversized, air-filled boxes or imperishable plastic armor.

- In a Gallup poll conducted for the Glass Packaging Institute in 1989, 72 percent of Americans said they would prefer to buy food or beverages in recyclable over nonrecyclable containers. If the product were

30

only offered in a nonrecyclable container, only 16 percent said they would keep buying it.

- The Washington Citizens for Recycling in Seattle, a nonprofit environmental group, recently praised and chastised marketers with a sort of Emmy Awards for packaging. Among the winners: the venerable cardboard egg carton, which is reusable, recyclable and even compostable; and the ice cream cone— the original edible package. Among the losers: "aseptic juice boxes," those little individually wrapped foil and cardboard packages, which are virtually impossible to recycle; and L'Eggs panty hose—those cute little plastic eggs are "clearly our Cadillac with fins," the group said. Another loser was the toothpaste pump: "When the paste is gone, there's the pump. You can't crush it. You can't refill it. Gotta toss it."

Says Ray Hoffman, executive director of the group: "We need to start evaluating packaging not only for its esthetic and promotional qualities but for whether the packaging is environmentally sound."

It's the sort of comment that tends to catch lawmakers' attention—especially when similar things are being said in every corner of the country. And legislators have been fast at work. In 1989, in state and local legislatures around the country, over 350 packaging-related proposals were introduced. Some of these proposals are an attempt to use the tax system to force any business which uses packing materials to either use recyclable material or pay taxes on materials that are not recyclable. A task force of legislators in the Northeast, where the garbage crisis is most acute, have recommended legislation aimed at completely

eliminating toxic substances from consumer packaging. The legislation will require companies to ana-
lyze their inks, dyes and other packing materials and
remove lead, chromium, cadmium, mercury and other
dangerous substances.

Pending legislation may also tax direct marketers
more, rather than less, for making heavy use of the
postal system, says industry analyst Roger Craver: "I
have no doubt it will be argued that those who mail
more, rather than qualifying for a discount on volume, should actually pay more for the 'waste' they
are putting into the system."

But industry has been listening to this "green revolution" among consumers, too. And dozens of companies in many different businesses are discovering
innovative ways to reduce the amount of packaging
they use, reduce the nondegradable materials they
use in their packaging, and make greater use of recycled materials. In the spring of 1990, the world wit-
nessed the first international conference on developing environmentally friendly packaging—Greenpak
90. Some ideas that emerged from this conference,
and elsewhere in industry, are spelled out here.

What You Can Do:

Go low tech. The most environmentally benign
packing materials are often the simplest ones, like
plain old newspapers, shredded computer paper or
cardboard. Seventh Generation ships even delicate
products like light bulbs in used, wadded-up computer paper, which can then be recycled by the recip-
ient. Or sometimes they use the leftover trimmings,

or roll ends, from web presses. "The printer is thrilled to get rid of them, and they give them to us free," says Seventh Generation's Alan Newman.

Some shippers have even begun using ordinary, air-popped popcorn, although Smith & Hawken, which started using popcorn a few years ago, had problems with ants. "I see other shippers starting to use popcorn again, and I'm afraid they're going to run into the same problem," says the company's environmental director Ted Tuescher.

On the horizon: High-tech low-tech packing materials. Vermont-based Earthright, for instance, is developing air-injected paper peanut pellets.

Nuts to you. There are now packing alternatives to those infernal, eternal polystyrene "peanuts," which not only contain ozone-depleting CFCs but also have a way of doing a timed-release explosion all over the customer's house after the box is opened. Due to its concern about the use of CFCs, Rodale quit using its old cushioning material several years ago and switched to FLO-PAK, a material made without CFCs by Free-Flow Packaging of Redwood City, California. This loose, lightweight material in a "figure eight" shape is made from 90 to 95 percent recycled polystyrene, and is the only recycled polystyrene made without CFCs. According to the company, other loose fill substances, like Dow Chemical's new Pelaspan-Pac, do contain CFCs in the blowing agents used.

Brown bag it. Seventh Generation used to ship some of its products wrapped in plastic, but now they've switched to cellophane or paper bags. "If you use things that would have looked funky only a year ago, like a paper bag—nicely printed with an explanation about why you're using paper instead of plastic—I doubt if you'd have a single customer who'd object," says Alan Newman. "My guess is you'd make a lot of friends." Cellophane, made from cellulose, is better than plastic, though not perfect, he adds. In the presence of light and air, it will degrade just like paper and can even be composted (although cellulose and almost everything else will not degrade in the anaerobic tomb of a landfill.) The sole manufacturer of cellophane in the United States is Flexel, of Atlanta, Georgia.

Smith & Hawken recently began shipping clothes in glassine bags. Glassine, used to make those crinkly, opaque envelopes for film negatives, is also made entirely of cellulose and should degrade in a landfill at the same rate as paper. It's not as moisture or rip-resistant as plastic, though, and the company is still experimenting with other substances. Something better than cellophane or glassine may be coming soon: "Bio-plastic starch," from Warner-Lambert. Stay tuned.

A whack on the side of the box. "One of the most obvious things shippers can do is simply try to use the smallest box possible, to save both corrugated cardboard and whatever packing material is used," says Rodale Press president Robert Teufel. "With enough demand from the marketplace, box manufacturers will increase the number of box sizes."

Adds Seventh Generation's Newman: "In your warehouse, you need to look at everything and say, 'Do I need this much packaging?' Most people I talk to say their customers want less. There was a day when more was better, but now we're in a day when less is better."

Sometimes lightening up the product you're shipping can be enough to reduce the packaging—and new developments in raw materials have hastened this development. Twenty years ago, a glass bottle was likely to weigh 11 ounces, but now it weighs only 9 and is equally strong. Since 1970, the typical soda bottle has dropped in weight from 60 to 40 grams, and is easier to crush.

Use recycled boxes. Try to use recycled corrugated boxes with as high a post-consumer waste content as possible. One good source for these and other environmentally benign packing materials is Maryland-based BioPax.

Reincarnate your boxes. At Seventh Generation, nearly all of the incoming corrugated boxes are reused in one way or another. Twenty percent of new merchandise is mailed out to customers in boxes that came into the warehouse filled with something else. These reincarnated boxes, which sometimes bear the logo of another company, are given a special stamp, to let people know that they have been reused and why.

Let's get small. What can you do to reduce the size of your product's package? "Source reduction by the packaging industry alone could take away 10 percent of the solid-waste stream," says Ed Fox, associate director of corporate packaging for Procter & Gamble. "It doesn't require any effort except for the packaging industry to 'get with it.' " Procter & Gamble has already vowed to reduce all its packaging by 25 percent. A newly-redesigned Crisco Oil bottle, for instance, now holds the same amount of oil with 28 percent less plastic.

Responding to consumer concern about packaging, a whole new category of "compact" products has also come on the market. Products like Procter & Gamble's "Ariel Ultra," a highly concentrated laundry detergent, which was first successfully tested in Germany, the world capital of the Green movement. Other products reduce packaging by combining two things, like detergent and colorfast bleach.

Can your package have life after death? Is there any way your product's packaging can be redesigned to be reused? After a ten-year absence from store shelves, Welch's recently reintroduced the venerable glass jelly jar that becomes a drinking glass once you've emptied its contents. All you throw away is the lid, which now bears all the printed information that would otherwise appear on a paper label. (Some of those wonderful old Welch's jelly jars from the '50s are now collector's items.) Grolsch beer, imported from Holland, comes in a handsome dark-green bottle with a wire-attached ceramic cap. The whole thing can be reused as an air-tight container for oil, vinegar or salad dressing.

Refill 'er up. A whole new wave of refillable product containers may soon be appearing on store shelves. In November 1989, for instance, Procter & Gamble began testing a program in which consumers buy "Downy Refill" fabric softener in the usual plastic container—but instead of throwing it away, reuse it. The next time they need Downy, they buy it in a pint-size cardboard box resembling a milk carton, a so-called "enviro-pak," mix it with water, and then refill the plastic jug. And why not? Who needs a plastic detergent jug, made for a single use, that's so imper-

ishable it will outlive your grandchildren? Four biodegradable refill packages take up about as much space
in a landfill as a single plastic jug.

Refillable packaging has already been very successful in Europe, and nearly every major marketer—
including Colgate-Palmolive, Dial and Unilever—has
plans to import its refillable packaging designs to the
United States. Says one industry observer, "For U.S.
consumers, the containers will look and perform dif-
ferently than anything they've ever seen."

Is there any way your company could do something
similar? At the Big Bear supermarket chain in San
Diego, for instance, grocery checkers pay two cents
for each plastic or paper bag a customer brings to the
store to reuse. And at U.S. retail stores of the innovative British cosmetics company, The Body Shop,
customers are encouraged to bring containers back
to be refilled.

Try sizzle substitution. Is it possible to reduce the
size of your package by substituting the sizzle of sheer
size with bolder graphics, or brighter colors, or more
ingenious marketing? Or by increasing the amount
of telemarketing you do? Or radio or TV advertising?
(Nice thing about TV: When you turn it off, there's
nothing to throw away.)

Do it in the nude. Is there any way you can get rid
of your packaging completely? Hammers or wrenches
often come in cardboard-backed, plastic-fronted
"blister packs." But if you're selling hammers, why
not just display them "in the nude," hung from a
pegboard or stacked in a tray like in the old days?
Shrink-wrapped tomatoes, apples or cucumbers, dis-
played on polystyrene trays, have to be some sort of

ultimate in useless packaging. As if Mother Nature hadn't already spent the past few million years working out the ideal packaging for a tomato!

In fact, nudist packaging—no packaging at all—is the very best solution to the solid waste crisis. "Source reduction" means that there's no waste in the first place, so you don't even have to worry about recycling it. Says "garbologist" Dr. William Rathje of Arizona University: "Source reduction is to garbage what preventive medicine is to health: a means of eliminating a problem before it can happen."

The Power of Purchasing: Buying a Better World

One of Smith & Hawken's mail order catalogues is devoted to lovely, expensive outdoor furniture, much of it made of teak. Ten or 20 years ago, few customers—and fewer companies—would have bothered to really wonder about the origins of that wood. Where did it actually come from? Did the teak harvest contribute to the destruction of the rain forest, the disappearance of species, the depletion of atmospheric ozone? What were the economic, environmental and political side effects of the logging operation? And so on.

Today, all environmentally aware companies need to begin asking questions like these, because the world is smaller now, more complex, more endangered. Companies need to consider not just the price and condition of goods arriving at the loading dock, but the entire "life cycle" of whatever it is they're buying. Because by learning to make conscious and careful purchasing decisions, companies can help to buy a better world.

When Smith & Hawken co-founder Paul Hawken became concerned about the source of the teak in his company's outdoor furniture a few years ago, he assigned a new employee, Ted Tuescher, to investigate the question and provide the company with enough information to make a responsible decision. Tuescher embarked on an 11-month journey into the jungles of international trade in exotic tropical hardwoods, ultimately making a trip to Southeast Asia to see for himself what was going on. He talked with foresters, journalists, environmentalists, United Nations officials, and expatriate researchers in Java, and reconstructed the whole history of British forestry in the Indian Empire.

One of the first things Tuescher discovered was that teak cutting doesn't endanger the rain forest because teak doesn't grow in rain forests. It's a sun-loving tree which grows only in the dry and semimoist forests of Southeast Asia; wet soils would cause its roots to rot.

But the answers to the other questions he asked were more complex. At the time he was hired, Smith & Hawken was buying furniture made mostly from Burmese teak. But Tuescher discovered that, though the Burmese claimed they were subscribing to a careful forest management system established by the British over a century ago—harvesting one teak tree per acre of forest every 30 years—in fact that was no longer true. Political turbulence in the region, desperate poverty, and a succession of military takeovers had destroyed the old system of sustainable forest management. Now the teak forest was being terribly overharvested, perhaps beyond its ability to recover. And the military government, which owned the forests, was using some of the profits to buy weapons that were being used against the Burmese people.

"We started out with what was primarily a concern about the environmental impact of the teak harvest, but the human rights abuses we discovered kind of pushed it over the edge," says Tuescher.

As a result of what he discovered, the company quickly switched to a new teak supplier in Java. There, the situation was quite different: It was simply too late to worry about saving the natural forests of Java, because they were already gone. Instead, since the 1860s, teak and other exportable hardwoods like mahogany and rosewood were grown on huge, government-operated tree plantations. The trees were cut in 60- to 80-year rotations, and with bud orchards and tissue culturing, the future health of this teak "forest" was assured. By buying teak from tree farms in Java, Smith & Hawken was in effect *encouraging* the growing of trees, not participating in their destruction. In the same way, they were supporting the human rights and aspirations of the local people, rather than destroying them, due to the many benevolent government programs funded by the sale of Indonesian teak.

But Smith & Hawken didn't stop with its own corporate decision to switch suppliers. Realizing that their research might be of use to other environmentally concerned businesses, the company made a $45,000 contribution to the New York–based Rainforest Alliance, to help set up a certification and labeling program for buyers of teak and other tropical hardwoods. That way, other companies would be able to purchase tropical wood with a clear conscience, and without going to all the trouble that Smith & Hawken did.

"By carefully choosing a source for our teak," the company told its customers in its spring, 1990 furniture catalogue, "we hope to encourage sustainable use of the environment as well as provide a valuable source of income for emerging economies that a ban on tropical woods would deny. . . .We want to do the best and most responsible job we can as a company and hope to do it with your support."

What You Can Do:

Become the market for recycled products. If your company is going to all the trouble of recycling paper, aluminum cans and glass, then you also need to become the market for the recycled products that are made from it. Purchasing recycled materials will stimulate demand, lower prices and support efforts to improve quality. But if there are no buyers for recycled products, recycling is a fruitless exercise. "If we're going to be a company that's putting all this recyclable material on the market, then we have a responsibility to help develop markets for it," Gail Mayville, environmental resources director at Ben & Jerry's, told *Harrowsmith* magazine. "Otherwise, we'll have a bunch of brokers with warehouses full of stuff."

Stay close to home. Try to find suppliers that are as close to home as possible. That way, you avoid excess shipping costs, conserve fuel, cut back on exhaust fumes, and support the local economy. It's not always possible to find close-to-home suppliers, admits Alan Newman, president of Seventh Generation—but you've got to try.

Ask suppliers to use less packing. There is a friendly way to ask your suppliers to use more environmentally benign packaging. Some companies have simply sent their suppliers a pleasant but explicit letter, requesting specific changes, such as substituting shredded paper for Styrofoam. Smith & Hawken, which has succeeded in getting hundreds of suppliers to change their packaging practices, sometimes actually sends its suppliers a sample package, to demonstrate what they're after. Lest they miss the point, the company has informed its suppliers that products packed in polystyrene peanuts will be sent back, as of June 1, 1991.

Buy in larger quantities. A good way to reduce unnecessary packaging is simply to buy in the largest quantities you possibly can.

Choke the yoke. Whoever buys food and beverages for the company cafeteria can do the Earth a favor by avoiding six-packs of canned drinks packaged in those infuriating plastic "yokes." As currently manufactured, most of them are nearly indestructible, and they're extremely dangerous to marine life. Floating on the surface of the sea, they look like translucent sea animals, and curious gulls, terns, pelicans, seals and sea lions often get them stuck around their necks, leading to slow starvation. (How could your six-pack ring possibly wind up in the ocean? Well, don't ask that question unless you know precisely where your office trash is dumped, and what happens to it afterward.) Institute a no-yoke company policy, as the Texas ad agency GSD&M did last year. Instead, order drinks in 12-can recyclable cardboard containers.

Don't make the fire any worse. Purchasing decisions for all kinds of in-house equipment, even fire extinguishers, can have a significant effect on the environment. When you're buying fire extinguishers, try to get the nonhalon type, which does not contain ozone-depleting CFCs.

Clean up the world when you clean up your office. What sort of stuff does the janitorial staff use on your office after you've gone home for the night? Nontoxic floor soap, toilet bowl cleaners and other environmentally benign products are available from AFM in Riverside, California. "Ecover" Earth-safe products are available at natural food stores or from their U.S. distributor, Mercantile Food.

The Ripple Effect: Energy Conservation As If The World Depended on It

Like a pebble plunked in a pond, every move your company makes sends out a ring of ripples—an expanding circle of consequences which affect the world in ways it's sometimes hard to imagine. Nowhere is this connection between local acts and global consequences more clear than in your company's use of electricity and (to a somewhat lesser extent) water.

The energy consumed by the light bulb you're using to read this page is almost certainly supplied by a faraway power plant, whose juice is produced by nuclear or hydroelectric power or by the burning of coal, oil or natural gas. One humble light bulb may not seem like much, but taken together, all the humble light bulbs in America consume 20 percent of the nation's entire electrical output. Just to keep the lights burning in all of America's businesses requires 100 billion-dollar, Chernobyl-sized power plants. Those power plants burn up about $24 billion in fuel each year—whether it's coal, natural gas, oil or nuclear—which in turn has a profound effect on the environment. Staggering amounts of carbon dioxide, the main "greenhouse gas," are belched into the atmosphere from power plants every day, not to mention all the other air emissions, water emissions, and solid waste they generate. Burning fossil fuels has geopolitical consequences, too, a fact of which Americans are made painfully aware every time the OPEC oil ministers light up their cigars and disappear into a hotel together in Baghdad or Riyadh.

Taken together, the ripples produced by all those little electric meters on all those little corporate headquarters extend around the world, affecting nearly all forms of life everywhere. Nobody's asking you to do without light or heat, of course. But there's a lot your company can do to live a little more lightly on the Earth.

What You Can Do:

Switch to compact fluorescents. The compact fluorescent light bulb is one of the most amazing breakthroughs in lighting technology in a long while, but lots of people still don't know about it. Energy guru Amory Lovins, research director of the Rocky Mountain Institute, sums up its wonders this way:

"A single 18-watt compact fluorescent light bulb produces the same light as a 75-watt incandescent bulb but lasts about 13 times as long. Over its lifetime, the new light bulb will slow global warming and reduce acid rain by avoiding emissions from a typical U.S. coal plant of one ton of CO_2 and about 20 pounds of SO_2 (sulphur dioxide). . . .The same fluorescent bulb will also save the cost of buying and installing a dozen ordinary bulbs (about $20); the cost of generating 570 kilowatt hours of electricity (about $20 + worth of fuel); and, during its lifetime, approximately $200–$300 worth of generating capacity."

Unlike old-fashioned fluorescent tubes, compact fluorescents don't flicker, hum, or make anybody who stands beside them look as if they've got an incipient case of malaria. The new-fangled fluorescents produce a warm, pleasant light (in fact, warmer and more pleasant than most incandescents.) Most of them will fit into an ordinary, old-fashioned socket. And they're much cooler, too. Conventional light bulbs convert only a fraction of their energy into light—10 percent for the typical incandescent, 30 percent for old-fashioned fluorescent tubes. The rest they turn into heat, further increasing your electric bill by putting an additional strain on ventilation and air conditioning. Because compact fluorescents convert so much more energy into light, they cut back on your cooling costs by as much as 5 to 20 percent.

Compact fluorescents cost more initially—$15 and up. But they will last for up to 10,000 hours, compared with the 750 hours of a typical incandescent bulb, so you come out way ahead in the long run. One thing to be careful of: There are already cheap imitations of the real thing on the market. Some of the reputable brands: Osram, Philips and Matsushita. You can identify the knockoffs, Amory Lovins told *Harrowsmith* magazine, because their boxes aren't labeled with how much light they put out or how long they last. If those two things aren't on the package, don't buy them.

The bottom line on compact fluorescents? Says Lovins: "Basically, you can improve the environment and make money on the deal." Who could ask for more?

Enter at the exits. A good place to start switching over to compact fluorescents is with your company's exit signs. Your average exit sign costs around $57 a year to operate, for electricity, new lights and maintenance. But by replacing the two 20- or 25-watt incandescents you'll find in there with a single compact fluorescent—which requires only 9 watts yet gives off as much light as a 40-watt incandescent—you can cut that cost down to $16 a year, says Robert Sardinsky, president of Colorado-based Rising Sun Enterprises, designers of energy-efficient lighting systems for business.

Smith & Hawken is in the process of retrofitting all their exit signs with compact fluorescent lights, a move the company expects will cut the energy they use by more than two-thirds. Easy-to-install kits are available for around $10 and will pay for themselves in energy savings within a year. Another good place to start: Safety and security lights, which burn up lots of energy because they're on all night. Kits are available from Easco, of West Conshohocken, Pennsylvania, and Oakland, California–based Wellmade.

Have an enlightening experience. It may be worth your while to have a complete "lighting audit" by a company versed in all the new lighting technologies now available, like Rising Sun Enterprises, of Snowmass, Colorado. (In addition to compact fluorescents, the company also uses clever little light-saving devices like sensors, which switch on the restroom lights only when somebody walks in the door.) These folks will come into your company and custom-design a whole system, using a whole array of new lighting technologies, to cut your energy costs in half (or better) while actually improving your lighting.

It can make an enormous difference. Typically, lighting accounts for 25 to 40 percent of the total energy use in a commercial building. But because utilities charge more for energy used during peak demand times (like regular business hours), those costs can actually go as high as 70 percent of your total electric bill. In most existing buildings, Rising Sun maintains, a lighting retrofit and redesign can trim your lighting bill by 40 to 60 percent, and pay for itself in around two years.

Taken together, the net effect of enhanced lighting efficiency can be amazing. Recently, for instance, Rising Sun did a lighting retrofit at Alpine Bank, a small bank next door to the company's headquarters. The total initial cost came to $6,200, but the projected annual energy savings came to $2,150. That means the return on investment was 34 percent, with a total payback time of 2.9 years. But the retrofit's contribution to the larger world is even more impressive. The bank saved 22,952 kilowatt hours of electricity a year, in the process conserving 22,953 pounds of coal which didn't have to be burned at the local power plant. As a result, the atmosphere was saved from 91,812 pounds of carbon dioxide and 597 pounds of sulphur dioxide emissions.

For more information, contact Rising Sun Enterprises or Rocky Mountain Institute at the addresses listed in the Directory.

It's a wrap. Elsewhere in your building, you should wrap your water heaters with insulation and keep them at an energy-conserving setting of 130°F. (Any lower, and there's a danger of bacterial contamination.) Every few months, drain off a few quarts from the bottom faucet to remove gunk and significantly increase the life of the tank.

Program your thermostat. It's also a good idea to install seven-day programmable thermostats, which cut back on your energy bill by regulating your building's heating to match the pattern of use. (Sure, somebody can always turn back the thermostat after the building is empty, but somebody always forgets.) Some utility companies give rebates for installing programmable thermostats, so check with yours.

Encourage car pooling. Try encouraging car pooling by setting up a free service in the company newsletter, matching up people who want to share the driving. Other companies have set up a van-pooling system, in which a company van is used as sort of mini bus line. Employees pay a small fee to offset the cost.

Rack 'em up. Encourage the use of bicycles by setting up bike racks around the company.

Get an electric car. Don't laugh—Smith & Hawken just bought a used electric vehicle from the U.S. Post Office for around $10,000. (The Post Office put 11,000 miles on it, but sold it because postal employees kept forgetting to recharge the thing.) It's a boxy little job with a range of about 50 miles, that will be used to shuttle back and forth between company buildings. For an additional $2500, solar panels were installed topside, to boost the life of the batteries. "It's the ideal solution for us," says company environmental director Ted Tuescher. "It's fairly inexpensive, it cuts down on emissions by over 90 percent. . . and when you're in it, all you hear is the wind." The company may even get a tax credit for using it. Their supplier: Solar Electric Engineering, of Rohnert Park, California, probably the only company in the U.S. actually selling electric cars.

But the big automakers are not far behind. In the spring of 1990, General Motors announced that it intends to be the first U.S. carmaker to mass-produce electric cars. To prove it, they trotted out a demonstrator model of a snazzy-looking two-seater called the Impact, which reportedly can out-accelerate many cars now on the road and has a top speed of 110 mph. The company declined to be too specific about price, but promised the cost would be "appealing." The main problem with the Impact and other electric cars, at least right now: They only have a range of about 120 miles, at which point the batteries have to be recharged for a couple of hours. (For commuters, or for company cars shuttling between locations, that would pose little problem at all.) Also, the lead-acid battery cells have to be changed after 20,000 miles, at a cost of around $1,500. Even so, one industry analyst says the total cost of operating the Impact would be only about three cents a mile more than a comparable gasoline-powered car—and after 40,000 miles, it would be the same.

At Ford and Chrysler, there are battery-powered vans now under development. Fiat is also working on a little two-seater called the Elettra, and at a recent auto show in Tokyo, Japanese auto makers had six different electric vehicles on display.

Clean, quiet and practical, electric cars seem like an appealing option for the greening corporation, especially in smog-choked cities like Los Angeles or Denver. But lawmakers may soon make them seem more than just practical. "Los Angeles officials, who often set the standards later adopted by other regions, now are drafting regulations that would prohibit businesses from opening their doors or expanding unless they offset any additional air pollution they might create," reports *U.S. News & World Report*. One way to meet that requirement: Replace gas-burning cars in the company fleet with electric vehicles. Companies might even encourage employees' use of electric cars by giving them special parking privileges—complete with outlets to recharge their batteries.

The electric car parking space may become the bike rack of the twenty-first century.

Water Wisdom

Hush that flush. Smith & Hawken has cut back on water waste by retrofitting their toilets with low-flush models that use only 1.5 gallons instead of the usual 3 to 5. They've been pleased with their Atlas model, made by Universal-Rundle of New Castle, Pennsylvania, which cost them $90. Retrofitting all the toilets at headquarters would be expensive, but there are some cheaper ways of saving water every time you flush. You can save 1 or 2 gallons per use by installing toilet dams, which are available in most hardware stores. You can also save 1 to 3 quarts per flush with the highly sophisticated and technical expedient of a plastic jug filled with stones, slipped into the toilet tank in such a way that it doesn't interfere with the flushing mechanism. Don't use the old brick-in-the-toilet trick, however, unless the brick is wrapped in a plastic bag. Bricks tend to disintegrate eventually, messing up the plumbing.

Give your faucets some air. You can cut the amount of water coming out of your faucets by 50 percent, and never know the difference, by installing low-flow faucet aerators or spray taps. These amazing little devices are widely available in hardware stores for less than $5 apiece. They're simple to install, too— you just screw them onto the threads on the end of the faucet. Normally, a tap will put out 3 to 5 gallons of water a minute, but these little jobs reduce the flow to as little as 2 gallons a minute. One simple trick to tell if you need an aerator: Hold a half-gallon bucket under the tap when it's turned on full force. If it fills in less than 10 seconds, it would pay to install an aerator. If you've got showers at work, it also helps to install low-flow shower heads (available for $10 or so), which can reduce the flow from 7 gallons a minute to about 2.

"Trash" Is a Dirty Word: Setting Up an In-House Recycling System

"If we'd known how easy it was to do this, I think we would have started it ten years ago," says Duane Elsasser, the self-proclaimed "Recycling King" at Rodale Press. "It's really not much trouble at all. In fact, I think it's one of the best things the company has ever done."

Although Rodale started recycling cardboard and paper scraps in its book-packing area about a decade ago, it was only during the summer of 1990 that a bona-fide, company-wide recycling program went into effect. It hasn't required hiring a "manager of recycling," an additional maintenance person—or anybody at all. It hasn't required buying a truck to move anything. The start-up costs were minimal (a few hundred bucks to build snazzy formica-surfaced disposal bins, though cardboard boxes would have worked as well.) It requires only a little bit of effort on the part of everybody. And it's enabled Rodale to recycle between 70 and 90 percent of its waste—at the same time it makes the company around $67,000 a year.

"The key is to keep it simple," says Special Projects Coordinator David Branton, who helped set up the program. Now, instead of chucking everything into the circular file, employees have a recycle container beside their desks: a cardboard box for the day's paper trash. Some also have a second box, for discarded newspapers and greenbar computer paper. The recycler Rodale uses can take almost any kind of paper— window envelopes, magazines, phone books, manila folders, colored paper, fax paper, the works. (This Hungarian goulash of paper is known as "office mix," and it's the lowest grade, so it generally brings the lowest price from recyclers. The highest grade is "sorted white ledger"—any kind of white, nonglossy office paper except for Kleenex or paper towels. To get a better price, you might consider sorting out your white paper and selling it separately.)

Each employee has the small additional task of taking his trash — aluminum cans, glass bottles, food waste, and the like—to the disposal bins located near rest rooms and cafeterias around the company. "The bins look sort of like those trash bins at McDonald's, except they have three slots, for glass, aluminum and trash," says Elsasser. "We went to a little expense to have them covered in a smooth formica finish, but we wanted them to look attractive and be visible." Adds Branton: "Once you've sorted out the paper, aluminum and glass, it's amazing how little is left to put in the 'trash' slot."

At the end of the day, the janitorial service makes its usual rounds, emptying the boxes from beneath everybody's desk and taking the contents to a central location in each building, where it's dumped in big cardboard "skid carts." The only difference is that now the trash is entirely paper—and it's not bound for the landfill. (In fact, it's not really trash at all.) When the skid carts fill up with paper, mail couriers—the people who deliver in-house mail to each of the company's 14 different buildings—load them on a pickup truck and drive them over to the operations center parking lot, where the recycler's 45-foot trailer truck is permanently parked. Once the trailer is brimful of paper—it holds 24 skid carts—the recycler comes and hauls it away to be sorted, bound, and eventually reused. (A similar system has been set up to recycle cardboard boxes.)

"We've been able to cut 200,000 pounds of paper a month out of our trash stream this way," says Elsasser. "We also save around $3,600 a month in trash-hauling fees, and the recycler pays us about $2,000 a month for the paper and cardboard. The company comes out $67,000 ahead."

Such are the testimonials of the Green Decade.

And there are thousands of them. The American Paper Institute estimates that American corporations now recycle 200,000 tons of paper a year. A decade ago, they recycled almost nothing. But it makes sense to do so, both financially and environmentally, as companies great and small have discovered.

- AT&T used to spend $1 million a year to have its trash hauled away. Now, after an in-house recycling program was instituted, they make $365,000 a year by selling it.
- In a 1989 cover story, *Time* magazine dubbed the Earth "Planet of the Year"... and then started

wondering what its own company was doing to honor the lady. An in-house recycling system was set up to collect bottles, cans and paper at its editorial offices in New York. Part of the money is donated to We Can, an organization that helps the homeless.

- At Sacred Heart Hospital in Allentown, Pennsylvania, simply taking cardboard out of the wastestream saved the institution $25,000 a year in trash hauling fees. Director of environmental services Robert Sweeney says the hospital cut its bill in half by compacting and baling cardboard; now the trash is picked up every ten days instead of every five. Sweeney convinced the hospital to buy a compactor, which paid for itself in six months.

- At the Coca-Cola Company in Atlanta, a corporate recycling system collects aluminum cans, white office paper, corrugated boxes, newspapers, phone directories, glass and containers made from PET plastic. Proceeds from the sale of all these reusable resources are donated to local charities, and amounted to $26,000 in 1988.

- If the Green Decade hasn't already inspired your company to begin recycling, don't worry. It's been a wonderful inspiration to lawmakers. New Jersey, Rhode Island and New York City have already passed laws requiring offices to recycle wastepaper.

What You Can Do:

Crown a king. The first thing you should do is put somebody in charge of setting up a system—crown a Recycling King, as it were. You don't have to hire anybody, just put somebody in charge. The job shouldn't require a lot of extra time, but it does require a certain devotion to the task. (Duane was a natural person to take the job at Rodale, because he was already in charge of the in-house mail delivery system, and mail couriers were the ones whose jobs were most affected by the new system. He also believed in its importance.)

The newly-crowned king should then set about organizing an "Environmental Task Force," a "Green Team," or whatever you'd like to call it. These folks then become responsible for setting up and monitoring the new program.

A few highly committed companies, like Ben & Jerry's and Patagonia, have hired full-time "environmental resource coordinators," who devote all their attention to minimizing the corporation's impact on the Earth. For most companies, this is probably not feasible, but it does have its advantages: A single individual can monitor the recycling program, search out suppliers of recycled materials, cut back on water and energy output, educate the staff, and set up an ongoing financial analysis of your whole environmental program.

Stage an invasion. It helps to set the program up as if you were staging an invasion: Have one general and lots of lieutenants. At TimeWarner in New York, there are 33 "floor captains" who each have responsibility for educating their coworkers on a single floor, and gently convincing them to participate. The same principle is used in a community recycling program in Durham, North Carolina, where "block captains" put up reminder signs and hand out containers. By spreading the authority, everybody gets involved, and nobody has to work too hard.

Keep it simple. "The more sorting, decision making or walking an employee must do, the less successful the program will be," says Mary Saltzman, a coordinator of the highly successful recycling program set up at the New Jersey offices of Bellcore (Bell Communications Research). What Bellcore discovered was that, despite their professed good intentions, many white-collar workers will balk at having to walk even a few steps to dump office paper into a hallway recycling container.

Some companies have set up a system where employees have a little folder on their desk, to be used as a receptacle for wastepaper. Once filled, the employee is supposed to take the folder into a nearby hall and chuck its contents into a recycling bin. But Bellcore's experience has shown that people just won't do it. Instead, the company set up a simple "two-can" system, in which there are two wastebaskets under each employee's desk, one for bona fide trash, the other for used office paper. You don't have to walk anywhere. You don't have to think about it. It doesn't take any time. All you have to do is alter your aim by 6 inches when you're consigning a memo to the circular file. (If you want to know if a company is really green, don't read the annual report. Just check to see if there are two trashcans under everybody's desk.)

Simple, sure—but it works. Bellcore has 8,300 employees, so providing everybody with an extra wastebasket, plus hallway receptacles for newspapers, cans and bottles, put a real strain on the petty cash drawer. But because the recycling program started saving the company $25,000 to $30,000 a month in garbage disposal fees, the initial capital costs of the program were paid for in three months. And the company managed to trim back its wastestream by an impressive 60 to 80 percent.

(Bellcore has started marketing a book/video presentation of its program, with advice on how to set it up, how to enlist corporate support and overcome objections, form a planning committee, and so forth. Contact the company at the address listed in the Directory.)

Recycle the Inc.'s ink. Ben & Jerry's, the Vermont-based makers of super-duper ice cream, has one of the most committed and complete in-house recycling programs we've seen. "The company's goal," says "Green Team" leader Gail Mayville, "is to be 100 percent involved in recycling, conservation, source reduction and avoiding disposables." Besides recycling all paper, cardboard and over 100,000 pounds of plastic a year, the company also has tried to stop throwing away ink. Laser printer toner cartridges, those cumbersome plastic monuments to our disposable culture, are refilled rather than thrown away. Many small companies can now provide this service. (Bellcore saved around $250,000 a year, and kept 5,000 to 10,000 toner cartridges out of the local landfill, by refilling them.) Printer ribbons are re-inked, rather than thrown away. Even office pens are refillable.

Roll the presses. For recycling to work, it's got to become a new habit of life. That means people have to be constantly, gently reminded—and rewarded—

for learning to do things in a greener way. Try starting a little newsletter (or just add a new department to the existing one, if you've got one) to keep employees abreast of what's going on with the recycling program.

At Lost Arrow, the parent company of Patagonia, a bright-eyed little rag called "Stinky Water Notes" keeps everybody informed about what's happening. There are notices about "recycling awareness teams," who meet once a month to discuss how the system is working and suggest improvements; general news about low-flow showerheads and energy-saving light bulbs; and monthly totals of how much waste has been kept out of landfills.

Don't do it in the dark. If you've got a photo lab, what are you doing to recycle darkroom chemicals? Some of them contain heavy metals, which can be very dangerous, especially to children. The Texas ad agency GSD&M bought a silver recovery filter system for $300, then found a local graphics company that would pick up the filter. The graphics company in turn sells the silver back to photographic companies, which reuse it.

And what about those little black plastic canisters that rolls of film come in? At Eddie Bauer, the Seattle-based marketer of outdoor clothing and equipment, thousands of the things were being discarded until somebody put in a call to Kodak to ask if the company would take them back. To everybody's surprise, Kodak was only too happy to. Now photographers who do work for the Eddie Bauer catalogue are asked to save the canisters and, once they've accumulated a boxful, ship them back to Kodak where they're cleaned, repackaged and reused.

Reuse the tubes. Smith & Hawken found a recycler to take their used fluorescent lights, which contain mercury (a hazardous material).

Make it pallet-able. Smith & Hawken also found a way to reuse wooden shipping pallets after they're damaged and "unusable." The company sells them to a cogeneration plant, where they're chipped and burned to generate electricity.

Get personal about it. Is there any way your company's recycling program can accommodate employee's personal trash? At Patagonia, the company provides employees with free Home Recycling Kits—attractive white cardboard boxes lined with reusable bags. You take a couple home, mark them "glass," "plastic," and "aluminum," and once you've got a bagful, bring the stuff in to work and dump it into the company's bins. One Patagonia outlet in Salt Lake City took this recycling largesse one step further and set up bins behind their store for people from the community to dump eight different kinds of recyclables there.

Set up a co-op. If you own or work for a very small business (as most people do), you might not generate enough recyclable waste for a recycler to take you seriously. So consider setting up some kind of recycling co-op with other small businesses in your area. Set up communal bins to collect the stuff, put all the proceeds into a communal fund, and then split it.

Hire an eco-entrepreneur. The Green Decade has spawned a new kind of eco-entrepeneur: the office recycling system consultant. These folks will come

into your company and, by working with management and local waste haulers and recyclers, set up a
complete system. One such company, Minnesota-based
Diversified Recycling Systems, also manufactures a
wide variety of recycling containers for office use,
from cardboard paper recycling files to compart-
mentalized plastic trash baskets and big, stackable
bins.

Try a little arithmetic. In one 11-month period,
employees of Patagonia used an amazing 2,350,000
sheets of copy paper. But it took the company's environmental resource coordinator, Tim Sweeney, to sit
down and figure that out—and then go tell everybody. Like the prospect of the gallows, a clean, simple
number like this can really steady a person's mind.
Try figuring out how much paper your company uses,
and post it around the company. Add these questions:
1. Did you proof this copy so there are no errors and
the copies will not have to be redone? 2. Can you
copy on both sides? 3. Do you really need to make
every copy that you plan to?

Awards! prizes! balloons! Be generous with praise
and awards when individuals, departments or the
whole company does something wonderful for the
Earth. In Patagonia's "Stinky Water Notes," people
are applauded for their success at home recycling—
like the employee who managed to throw away only
one bag of trash in a whole week. Another notice
gave a cheer to the company for having switched to
recycled stationery and copy paper, thereby saving
315 trees a year. Or picture this: Instead of those
posters of a giant thermometer, depicting the progress
of the United Way's latest fund drive, how about

some sort of Green-O-Meter, showing the company's success at cutting down their wastestream. We're at 55 percent, heading for 80!

Be your company's recycling hero. Every company needs somebody who gets it all started—and it's not necessarily top management. All it takes is a little passion, a little nerve, and an unwillingness to quit. In your company, why can't it be you?

Let It Green

Trimming back paper waste, recycling, using less packaging—they're all ways of saving the earth *indirectly*. They're ways of living lightly, of minimizing your corporate impact on the biosphere. But sometimes it's simpler and more soul-satisfying to take bold, direct action. Salute the Earth with a shovel and plant a tree, for instance. Or set up a corporate wildlife refuge—even if it's only a humble patch of uncut meadow out behind the office. Or just give the birds a break by banning the use of pesticides on your corporate turf.

What You Can Do:

Plant a corporate tree
"Fundamental facts of nature have convinced a number of experts that widespread planting of trees, along with conservation of existing forests, is one of the surest, easiest and least expensive ways to begin to halt or even reverse the buildup of carbon dioxide in the air," reports the *New York Times*.

Why does that matter? It matters because CO_2 is by far the most important of the "greenhouse gases,"

the mostly man-made emissions which are believed
to be responsible for global warming. The burning of
fossil fuels sends millions of tons of carbon aloft into
the atmosphere every year. But growing trees absorb
CO_2, storing the carbon part of the gas and releasing
the rest as oxygen. Trees use carbon to build plant
tissue and sustain their own lives, while nourishing
all other forms of life that require oxygen to breathe.
This great wheel of life, called the "carbon cycle,"
has been disturbed by human civilization in two dia-
bolically interconnected ways: We send fantastic
amounts of carbon into the atmosphere at the same
time we're deforesting the earth at a fantastic rate,
thus choking off its ability to reabsorb all that carbon.
In the tropics, an estimated 27 million acres of trees
are destroyed every year. Worldwide, only one tree
is planted for every four that are cut down.

As a consequence, the atmosphere appears to be
heating up at an alarming rate. The 1980s produced
the five hottest years on record. And over the past 20
years, the average rate of global warming has been
three times higher than had been predicted by cli-
matologists. But companies can do a great deal to
help in the releafing of the Earth, and a vast array of
American corporations already have.

- Many companies, such as Dow Chemical and the
  Geo division of Chevrolet, have funded large-scale
  tree plantings.
- Other companies have responded to the "offset"
  strategy suggested by some environmentalists:
  Companies should replace as many trees as it takes
  to absorb the carbon dioxide their operations produce. In one model effort of this kind, the Con-

necticut utility AES Thames is helping to pay for the planting of 52 million trees in Guatemala. The company calculates that the trees will absorb enough carbon to offset the atmospheric carbon produced by a new generating plant the company is building in Connecticut.

- The "Green Pages" campaign is a variant on this idea: Magazine publishers pledge to plant as many trees as it took to produce their periodicals. *New Age Journal*, for example, recently announced plans to plant between 5,000 and 10,000 trees. Eight other titles say they'll follow suit, including *Parenting, Utne Reader, Greenpeace Magazine, Buzzworm* and *Orion Nature Quarterly*. Along similar lines, the direct marketer Smith & Hawken has announced its intention to plant two seedlings for each tree the company uses for paper pulp in their catalogues—and to nurture the little trees until they're self-sufficient.

- One of the most ambitious tree-planting programs is the American Forestry Association's "Global ReLeaf" campaign, whose aim is to plant 100 million new trees in American cities and towns by 1992. Your company can become involved in this program, either in a very modest way (such as distributing brochures or running public service announcements) or in a very big way (by providing financial support or distributing seedlings directly to customers). So far, about 100 corporations have become involved in one way or another. Gardener's Supply, the direct marketer of gardening equipment, donates a percentage of its sales of one product (a shredder/chipper) to Global ReLeaf. Rodale Press advertises the campaign's 900 number and runs PSAs. And the Safeway grocery store chain has printed and distributed over 13 million (recycled) paper grocery bags with the Global ReLeaf message.

With its usual world-conquering style, McDonald's also joined the campaign with a massive initiative, in which an estimated 8 million trees are to be planted around homes, schools and offices in 1990. The company first sent educational material to local elementary schools in test markets, then distributed seedlings free to customers through its restaurants. The tiny trees, planted in recycled polystyrene pots, came with step-by-step instructions for transplanting into the ground four to six weeks later.

For more information, contact the American Forestry Association at the address listed in the Directory.

Start a wildlife sanctuary. In the early 1970s, when the chemical manufacturing business was little regulated, people who lived near an Air Products and Chemicals plant near Pensacola, Florida, began noisily objecting to fish kills in the nearby bay. At that time, the Escambia plant was producing 8 million gallons of effluent a day from the production of ammonia, amines and other chemicals.

In 1973, the company responded by establishing the Escambia Wildlife Sanctuary, in cooperation with the Florida Game and Freshwater Fish Commission. This 1,200-acre preserve, which surrounds the plant grounds, centers around five water quality control ponds, which process effluent from the plant. In an effort to comply with new federal water quality standards, satisfy the neighbors and be good environmental citizens, the company gradually reduced the amount of effluent from 8 to 1 million gallons a day, and improved the purity of its wastewater to the point where birds began congregating around the ponds in great numbers. The president of the local Audubon Society began leading field trips through the area, and over the years has identified 268 bird species there. A couple of Eagle Scouts blazed a nature trail through the park, complete with markers identifying plants and shrubs. A nature guide has been printed up, and now birdwatchers and boy scouts come from all over the state to visit.

Setting up your own wildlife sanctuary is an ambitious undertaking. But other companies have also become protectors of untamed places by making financial contributions to groups which preserve threatened or ecologically important land. In 1987, for instance, Smith & Hawken, the direct marketers of tools and gardening supplies, made a $100,000 contribution to Conservation International. The money went to preserve a precious piece of the biosphere in Costa Rica. In 1988, the company made a $700,000 contribution to the San Francisco-based Trust for Public Lands, to preserve an unspoiled stretch of Nevada's Ruby Mountains which had been scheduled for development. Later, the company ran an announcement of the purchase in its catalogue, along with a few delicious photographs of this wild, golden place. "A Gift from You to You," the headline read. It was the company's way of presenting this piece of the world's wildness to its customers, since "they were really the ones who allowed us to do it," says Smith & Hawken environmental director Ted Tuescher.

What's that you say? Seven hundred grand sounds a trifle steep? Well, how about adopting a field or a bit of woods somewhere around the home office? For years, Rodale Press has simply left a small field outside its main building completely uncut. The meadow has a shaggy magnificence which changes with each passing season, and is much more interesting to look at than an ordinary lawn. It also provides habitat for butterflies, bees, spiders, meadow voles and a certain beady-eyed black cat.

The rest of the lawns at Rodale are allowed to grow a little longer than most people are accustomed to seeing them, which saves both the fuel the mowers use and the pollution they cause. No fertilizers or pesticides are used, either, keeping the water table free of poisons and giving the birds, insects and animals one less reason to move to Wyoming.

Pick a Project, Any Project

There are any number of ways your company can help lead the way into a better, greener world. You can start with little things, like setting up an in-house composting system, or helping round up volunteers for a local nonprofit environmental group. Or you can start with the big things, like recycling an old building instead of putting up a new one, or tithing a small percentage of your profits to green causes. It doesn't have to hurt. It doesn't even have to cost much. All that matters is that you do something.

What You Can Do:

Recycle buildings. If your company is going to the trouble of recycling aluminum cans and copy paper, why not bricks, boards and shingles? When you "recycle" an old building rather than put up a new one, you're conserving resources—sometimes lovely, irreplaceable ones like solid oak doors or slate stairways—that would otherwise have to be manufactured out of virgin materials. You may save a sage old tree that would have been cut to make way for a new building. And you're fitting more calmly and naturally into the human environment of your community.

Most of the thousand employees of Rodale Press are housed in one of 13 buildings scattered around the little town of Emmaus, Pennsylvania. All but a couple of these structures are old buildings—some of them dating back to the late nineteenth century— that were renovated to suit the needs of twentieth-century corporate life. There are a couple of converted silk mills, an old cigar factory, an elementary school, a historic farm, and a few single family houses.

The cigar factory, which now houses the book division editorial staff, had been used most recently as a furniture warehouse and was in decrepit condition when the company bought it. As the renovation proceeded, there were wonderful discoveries. The whole top deck turned out to be golden oak, for instance— a grove of oaks, long since brought to earth, that would be preserved so that living oaks could be saved.

"We weren't in any big rush, so we went slowly. We worked by feel," recalls Ardath Rodale, the company's environmental resources director. A reception area was added, then conference rooms, a lunch room, offices, an elevator. The intent was to combine the best of the old world and the new, and to use existing materials wherever possible. Upstairs, it would have been nice to use cedar shipped in from the West Coast. But elsewhere on the company's property, a small stand of oaks had been taken down to make way for a power line, so the oak was kiln-dried and transformed into windowsills. By using local materials, and local craftsmen, the company recycled available materials, saved trees from the saw, cut down on shipping costs, truck fumes and wasted fuel, and employed local people.

From the Earth's point of view, it's cheaper to renovate old buildings than to use new materials. But what does it look like on the corporate P&L sheet? "The cost of renovating an old building, compared to building a new one, really depends on the condition of the existing building," says architect Howard Kulp, who has been involved in many of the Rodale renovations. The cigar factory transformation probably cost 10 or 15 percent more than building a new building, Kulp says, partly because "there were some problems we had to negotiate, like heavy old beams." Other renovations have cost about the same as, or less than, building from scratch.

There are tangible benefits to be gained from treating buildings as a renewable resource. In an old building, says Mrs. Rodale, it's often easier to illuminate work spaces with natural light than it is in modern buildings, because of the massive old windows and skylights. One of the renovated silk mills has a "sawtooth roof" common to factories of the nineteenth century—a series of steeply-pitched glass roofs which produce a jagged silhouette as well as an abundance of natural light. Built in a day of seemingly unlimited resources, old buildings also tend to have a massiveness which would be prohibitively expensive to recreate from scratch. Though the renovated cigar factory stands 40 feet from a busy railroad line, the old brick walls are so thick they're nearly soundproof. (How many twentieth-century bricks would it take to build a brand-new sound-absorbing wall?) And, though old buildings tend to be inadequately insulated, there are modern methods of solving that problem economically. In several of the renovations, an attractively-surfaced beaded styrene insulation has been applied to the exterior of the existing brick walls, resulting in what looks like stucco surfacing. It's a way of having the best of both worlds: twentieth-century energy efficiency and environmental friendliness, plus nineteenth-century charm.

Don't be cruel to animals. Does your company use or market any products which are tested on animals, such as cosmetics or pharmaceuticals? Many environmentally aware companies, like The Body Shop and Amway, have foresworn the use of animal-tested products, rejecting such tests as cruel and unnecessary. Nearly every page of The Body Shop's direct mail catalogue of natural skin and hair care products is boldly stamped with the words "Against Animal Testing." Instead, the company makes use of what it considers more meaningful and appropriate alternatives—extensive testing on human volunteers, and nonanimal laboratory tests. The company also supports new alternatives to animal testing for cosmetics.

Amway has also stopped marketing animal-tested products, as well as other products it considers environmentally harmful (including one caustic drain cleaner that was a multimillion-dollar item). As company spokesman Casey Wondergem told the *Chicago Tribune*: "If you brag about how green you are, you had better be green from head to toe."

Let it rot. If you serve food to employees, what happens to all those leftover coffee grounds, watermelon rinds and half-eaten sandwiches? By setting up a simple composting system, you can use it to nourish the earth which provided all that food in the first place—and maybe even grow more food.

The in-house food service at Rodale Press has had a composting program in place for years. In the company kitchens, organic waste and paper waste are dumped into separate buckets, explains Rodale Food Service Director Tom Nye. Since the company feeds around 800 employees a day in its five cafés, that amounts to something like 40 gallons of choice, compostable food waste daily. The buckets of organic waste, covered and set out by the dumpsters behind the kitchen, are picked up twice a week by staffers from the Rodale research farm. At the farm, the waste is dumped into composting bins, where it's combined with leaves, grass clippings and the good offices of a few billion tiny organisms, which break it all down into nutrient-rich, aerated soil. This choice, composted soil is then used as nourishment for the fruit and vegetable gardens—which produce two or three deliveries of fresh food a week during growing season, Nye says.

It's a sort of earth-to-earth, "closed loop" system, simple and efficient, in which food waste eventually winds up producing more food.

Despite its practical simplicity, composting is a profound natural process, part of nature's great cycle of endless renewal. It may also hold the key to a genuine solution to the solid waste crisis. Procter & Gamble has been doing some intriguing work with industrial-scale composting, in which plastic, glass and metal are sorted out of the trash stream and the rest—food, paper, cardboard and everything else—is dumped into enormous, revolving cylinders. Then it's slow-cooked. With the help of oxygen, bacteria and heat, what we think of as trash eventually emerges as the world's most precious renewable resource: rich, black dirt.

Give at the office. Direct financial contributions to environmental causes are one of the simplest ways for companies to help save the Earth. Amway, for instance, recently contributed $500,000 to the formation of an environmental think tank called the Aspen Institute for Global Change. Other companies, like Ben & Jerry's and Patagonia, consider contributions to environmental and social causes to be one of the central reasons for their existence as companies. Ben & Jerry's contributes 7.5 percent of its pretax profits to green causes, and Patagonia's "corporate tithing program" supports the efforts of over 250 organizations on a variety of environmental issues. The company devotes a breathtaking 10 percent of its pretax profits to nonprofit organizations; just keeping track of all these contributions requires one full-time employee.

Smith & Hawken recently sponsored a benefit to raise money for the video, *Rainforests: Proving Their Worth*, which demonstrates the economic value of nontimber products from the tropical rain forests of the Amazon. The program shows that it's possible for people to earn a living in these areas without cutting down the forests, such as doing business in fruits, nuts, oils, fiber and other forest products. In this way, Smith & Hawken throws its financial weight onto the side of a sustainable rain forest economy, rather than one based upon slashing, burning and waste.

Encourage volunteerism. "There are lots of ways to contribute financially to environmental causes, but we thought there were probably people who wanted to become more directly and personally involved," says Catharine Hartnett, a spokeswoman for L. L. Bean. "People who really wanted to learn about conservation and really see the results of their work. People who asked, 'What can I do to help instead of just writing a check?' "

At the same time, she says, many company employees were personally involved in doing volunteer work for conservation groups in Maine—maintaining trails, cleaning river banks, picking up campgrounds and state parks. Many of these nonprofit groups suffered from a shortage of volunteer troops to carry out the dirty work of sprucing up the world.

So the idea for "OVO"—Outdoor Volunteer Opportunities—was born. Bean's idea was to create a sort of environmental dating service, matching needy conservation groups with willing volunteers in their area. First the company drew up a list of conservation groups across the United States and Canada, then checked with them to see if they could put volunteers to work. Then they ran notices in selected Bean catalogues, explaining the program and inviting readers to contact the company for more information. Those who did—and so far, 3,500 people have—were sent a list of environmental groups in their area who would be only too happy to hear from them.

"This is not just advocacy work, this is 'dirty fingernails' stuff—but it's something a whole family could get involved in," says Hartnett. "Dedicated volunteers are needed at the grass roots level, so we felt this was a meaningful and responsible way for the company to make a contribution. We're contributing volunteers."

Conserve your human resources. A company's most important resource is its people, says Robert Teufel, president of Rodale Press. If the emerging corporate ethic of the Green Decade is a new honor and concern for the world's natural resources, it's time that companies learned to bestow the same gentle favors on their own people. Too often, companies have treated employees like any other disposable American invention—to be used up and then thrown away.

Rodale's corporate fitness programs, its incentives to keep people active through walking and running, and a company-wide no-smoking policy treat employees as a resource which needs to be cared-for, conserved, renewed. Employees are offered the use of company garden plots, to grow their own food; and the company subsidizes the in-house food service, so that nutritious meals can be had at a reasonable price. Such policies manifest a new ideal: Conservation of people is as important, perhaps more important, than the conservation of air, land or water.

Become a teacher. It's important for companies who've become environmentally aware, or just learned a few new tricks about how to bring corporate practice into line with environmental conviction, to share the news. Many committed companies do feel an obligation to become environmental educators—of their customers, suppliers, vendors, business associates and other members of their trade associations. And that's as it should be.

At Eddie Bauer, the Seattle-based marketer of outdoor clothing and equipment, the company has turned parts of its catalogue, sides of packing boxes and other printed materials into classroom handouts on environmental awareness, says company advertising director Marsha Savery. Brief messages explain the value of recycling or describe the damage that trailside litter can do to a mountainside. "It's a way of raising environmental consciousness, but not in a dictatorial or condescending way," says Savery.

The company's role as teacher really began, she says, as a "groundswell" of concern from employees. It was the employees—many of them enthusiastic campers and hikers attuned to the abundant natural glories of the Pacific Northwest—who began pushing for more environmentally benign corporate practices. "They'd say, 'Sure, we recycle paper and aluminum, but what about plastic bags and hangtags? What about darkroom chemicals?' " Savery recalls. "Then a task force would be set up to deal with plastics and darkroom chemicals."

The zeal and commitment of the staff was eventually transmitted to the company's customers all over the country. And, in retrospect, this seems a right and proper way to do things. "After all, education begins at home," says Savery. "We kind of started on the inside, and worked our way out. We just felt that if we were environmentally responsible, it would rub off on our customers. I mean, how can we get customers to do good things for the environment, if we don't do them ourselves?"

Become a company of principle. The astounding speed with which a giant twentieth-century corporation can desecrate the Earth was unforgettably demonstrated during the 1980s, when, within hours, the wreck of the *Exxon Valdez* turned one of Alaska's wildest and most pristine ocean inlets into a sea of deadly, stinking goo. But these events did not go unnoticed, or unmourned. For many people, the *Exxon Valdez* incident was a vivid demonstration of the need for corporations to bravely and publicly stand up for business practices which preserve the Earth, not just grudgingly accede to the latest round of government regulations.

In September of 1989, a coalition of concerned environmental groups, churches, labor unions, socially responsible investment groups and others unveiled a sort of Ten Commandments of environmentally responsible corporate behavior. This list of ten pledges, called the "Valdez Principles," were to be signed by corporations who wished to publicly affirm their commitment to environmentally sound business practices.

"Our intent is to create a voluntary mechanism of corporate self-governance that will maintain business practices consistent with the goals of sustaining our fragile environment for future generations, within a culture that respects all life and honors its interdependence," the group stated. Known as CERES, for Coalition for Environmentally Responsible Economies, the group includes the Sierra Club, Friends of the Earth, the National Audubon Society, the Social Investment Forum, Working Assets Money Fund, the Calvert Social Investment Fund, and others, representing more than 10 million people and $150 billion in invested assets.

Signatories of the Valdez Principles are asked to file an annual CERES report, explaining and discussing their achievements in complying with the Principles. There's also an annual fee, based on revenues. (Example: A company with annual revenues of $10 to $50 million pays $500 a year.) The Valdez Principles are a succinct summation of many of the things which have been discussed in this book, and an expression of values to which all corporations may one day aspire.

The Valdez Principles:

1. *Protection of the Biosphere*
We will minimize and strive to eliminate the release of any pollutant that may cause environmental damage to the air, water or earth or its inhabitants. We will safeguard habitats in rivers, lakes, wetlands, coastal zones and oceans and will minimize contributing to the greenhouse effect, depletion of the ozone layer, acid rain, or smog.

2. *Sustainable Use of Natural Resources*
We will make sustainable use of renewable natural resources, such as water, soils and forests. We will conserve nonrenewable natural resources through efficient use and careful planning. We will protect wildlife habitat, open spaces and wilderness, while preserving biodiversity.

3. *Reduction and Disposal of Waste*
We will minimize the creation of waste, especially hazardous waste, and wherever possible recycle materials. We will dispose of all wastes through safe and responsible methods.

4. *Wise Use of Energy*
We will make every effort to use environmentally safe and sustainable energy sources to meet our needs. We will invest in approved energy efficiency and con-

servation in our operations. We will maximize the
energy efficiency of products we produce and sell.

5. *Risk Reduction*
We will minimize the environmental, health and
safety risks to our employees and the communities
in which we operate by employing safe technologies
and operating procedures and by being constantly
prepared for emergencies.

6. *Marketing of Safe Products and Services*
We will sell products or services that minimize
adverse environmental impacts and that are safe as
consumers commonly use them. We will inform customers of the environmental impacts of our products
or services.

7. *Damage Compensation*
We will take responsibility for any harm we cause
to the environment by making every effort to fully
restore the environment and to compensate those
persons who are adversely affected.

8. *Disclosure*
We will disclose to our employees and to the public
incidents relating to our operations that cause environmental harm or pose health or safety hazards. We
will disclose potential environmental, health or safety
hazards posed by our operations, and we will not
take any action against employees who report any
condition that creates a danger to the environment
or poses health and safety hazards.

9. *Environmental Director and Managers*
We will commit management resources to imple-
ment the Valdez Principles, to monitor and report
upon our implementation efforts, and to sustain a

process to ensure that the Board of Directors and Chief Executive Officer are kept informed of and are fully responsible for all environmental matters. We will establish a Committee of the Board of Directors with responsibility for environmental affairs. At least one member of the Board of Directors will be a person qualified to represent environmental interests to come before the company.

10. *Assessment and Annual Audit*

We will conduct and make public an annual self-evaluation of our progress in implementing these Principles and in complying with applicable laws and regulations throughout our worldwide operations. We will work toward the timely creation of independent environmental audit procedures which we will complete annually and make available to the public.

If your company wishes to become a signatory to the Valdez Principles, or if you simply want to find out more, contact CERES at the address listed in the Directory.

It may be that your company's corporate officers, board of directors or shareholders do not feel comfortable putting their names to this agreement. If that's the case, is there any way your company could articulate—and lay down in writing—its own principles of environmental responsibility? Even if it's only a private agreement, with a signatory of one, doing so might help your company clarify its environmental goals, and perhaps even become one of the torchbearers of our passage into a better, greener world.

Directory of Green Products and Services

Now that you know what *can* be done, here's a list of suppliers to help you get started. It is by no means a complete list of the products available or the suppliers of those products and services. It is intended to serve as a starting point for putting into action some of the ideas presented in this book. With technology changing rapidly, the list of environmental entrepreneurs is constantly growing.

Cleaning Products

AFM Enterprises, Inc.
1140 Stacy Ct.
Riverside, CA 92507
714-781-6860
Nontoxic floor soap, toilet cleansers and other products specifically designed for use with the chemically ill and environmentally sensitive

Clean Environments, Inc.
P.O. Box 17621

Boulder, CO 80308
303-494-1770
Nontoxic, concentrated all-purpose cleaner

Goode Chemical Co., Inc.
350 E. Orangethorpe Ave. #1
Placentia, CA 92670
714-993-3279
Biodegradable, water-based cleaners and degreasers

Mercantile Food Co.
P.O. Box 1140
Georgetown, CT 06829
203-544-9891
"Ecover" floor soap, toilet cleaner, dishwashing liquid, nonabrasive cream cleaner and other products

Orange-Sol, Inc.
955 N. Fiesta Blvd.
Gilbert, AZ 85234
1-800-877-7771
Citrus-based cleaning products made from orange peels

Consultants

Bellcore
Room 4D114
290 W. Mt. Pleasant Ave.
Livingston, NJ 07039
1-800-527-1080
Book/video presentation of Bellcore's recycling system

Corporate Recycling, Inc.
200 31st St.
Boulder, CO 80303
303-499-3243
Designers of office recycling and waste-reduction programs

Energy-Saving Equipment
325 DeBaliviere #144
St. Louis, MO 63112
314-862-5067
Energy-efficient lighting consultants

Matlack Environmental Resources
4201 University Dr.
Suite 102
Durham, NC 27707
919-383-6265
Designers of commercial/office recycling programs

Rising Sun Enterprises, Inc.
P.O. Box 586
Old Snowmass, CO 81654
303-927-8051
Designers of energy-efficient lighting systems

Energy Systems/Products

Easco
5 Portland Rd.
West Conshohocken, PA 19428
215-828-5060
Kits for retrofitting exit lights, downlights and other light fixtures with compact fluorescent light bulbs

Energy Concepts Co.
627 Ridgely Ave.
Annapolis, MD 21401
301-226-6521
Industrial energy conservation systems

North American Philips Lighting Corp.
Philips Square
200 Franklin Square Dr. CN6800
Somerset, NJ 08873
201-563-3000
Compact fluorescent light bulbs

Sunsign Manufacturing Company
2002 Mendel Pl.
Swearingen Research Park
Norman, OK 73069
405-329-5993
Solar-powered outdoor signs

The Watt Watcher
296 Brokaw Rd.
Santa Clara, CA
1-800-879-8585
Infrared and ultrasonic occupancy and motion sensors and other automatic light switches

Office Products/Services

Black Lightning
RR #1-87
Depot Rd.
Hartland, VT 05048
802-436-3257

Remanufactured toner cartridges for laser printers, recycled paper for laser printers. Will accept used toner cartridges for recycling.

Diversified Recycling Systems
5606 N. Highway 169
New Hope, MN 55428-3099
612-536-6828
Office recycling system consultants; also offer a full line of products for office and warehouse recycling systems

Melitta North America
1401 Berlin Rd.
Cherry Hill, NJ 08003
609-428-7202
Unbleached coffee filters

Rockline, Inc.
Box 1007
1113 Maryland Ave
Sheboygan, MI 53801
414-458-7759
Unbleached coffee filters

Soft Dimensions, Inc.
201 W. Manville St.
Compton, CA 90224
1-800-658-0322
The Economy Diskette Drawer, a bulk storage unit made from recyclable corrugated cardboard

Packaging

Biopax
Diversified Packaging Products, Inc.
1265 Pine Hill Dr.
Annapolis, MD 21401
301-974-4411
Recycled corrugated boxes and other products made with recycled or degradable materials

Deltapaper Corporation
2925 State Rd.
Croydon, PA 19020
215-788-1800
Packing and wrapping materials that are either recyclable or made from recycled materials

Ecopak Industries, Inc.
7859 S. 180th St.
Springbrook Bldg. 3
Kent, WA 98032
206-251-0918
Cellulose bags and sheets and brown kraft paper packing materials

Free-Flow Packaging
1093 Charter St.
Redwood City, CA 94063
1-800-888-9946
FLO-PAK recycled polystyrene packing material

MBX Company
P.O. Box 929
Wausau, WI 54401
715-845-1171
Pallets, crating, and packaging made from HDPE

Recycled Paper

Conservatree Paper Company
10 Lombard St. #250
San Francisco, CA 94111
415-433-1000
Recycled paper products

Cross Pointe Paper Corp.
1295 Bandana Blvd. N.
Suite 335
St. Paul, MN 55108
1-800-543-3297
Recycled book-publishing grades, white and colored offset, cover stock

Fort Howard Paper Company
P.O. Box 19130
Green Bay, WI 54307
414-435-8821
Unbleached 100 percent post-consumer toilet tissue

James River Paper Company
P.O. Box 2218
Richmond, VA 23217
804-644-5411
Recycled toilet tissue

Georgia-Pacific Corp.
P.O. Box 105605
Atlanta, GA 30348-5605
404-521-4000
White and colored offset, computer printout paper,
office forms

Water Conservation

Mini Flush Company, Inc.
3960-K Prospect Ave.
Yorba Linda, CA 92686
1-800-969-0693
Water conservation device for toilets

Universal-Rundle
P.O. Box 29
New Castle, PA 16103
412-658-6631
Low-flush toilets

Water Conservation Systems, Inc.
9 Pond Ln.
Concord, MA 01742
508-369-3951
Compost and low-flush toilets and water savers

Water Control International, Inc.
51155 Grand River Ave.
Wixom, MI 48096
1-800-533-3460
Flushmate, a water-conserving tank operating system

Environmental Organizations

American Forestry Association
P.O. Box 2000
Washington, DC 20013
202-667-3300

CERES
711 Atlantic Ave., 5th Floor
Boston, MA 02111
617-451-0927

Friends of the Earth
218 D St. SE
Washington, DC 20003
202-544-2600

National Audubon Society
950 3rd Ave.
New York, NY 10022
212-832-3200

Rocky Mountain Institute
1729 Snowmass Creek Rd.
Snowmass, CO 81654-9199